Trauma Bonds

poems about our shared human and
American experience

Paulomi Dholakia

BookLeaf
Publishing

India | USA | UK

Made with ❤ on the BookLeaf Publishing Platform

www.bookleafpub.in

www.bookleafpub.com

Dedication

For those who have always encouraged my voice to be heard

&

Mr. Griffith, my 10th grade English teacher, who in a school that saw me as the nerdy scientist, told me I should just become a troubadour poet.

Preface

I have been writing poetry since I was five years old, but never did I think I would be publishing some myself. These poems contain more recent thoughts and reworked ones from the confines of my journal, spanning back the last ten plus years. They are meant as a means to remind you regardless of the trauma life may have given you, you are not alone.

Acknowledgements

Thank you first off to my parents for giving me this American life where I can do anything - like write poetry - and for being the support I need even as a grown adult. Thank you to my sister, a poet herself, for encouraging me to follow my passions and being my biggest cheerleader.

I would have never started writing again if it were not for someone who saw me so clearly and reminded me that I am an artist despite my self- deprecation and anxiety. You know who you are. Thank you so much.

waiting

I was once young too
a child in class learning
about the waves and the moon
the earth and erosion
and how we poked a hole in the sky
with our disrespect
for mother Earth

and now I am an adult
bound by society's chains
of policy and legality
and confusion and fear
watching as she burns

I am complacent it seems
for I know she is sick
I know I partake in poison
but in this world run by the wealthy
I am poor and small

and am convinced daily
that my views in life
don't reflect my own humanity
but are defined solely

by which politician
agrees outwardly
though i know behind closed doors
they are all the same

corrupt
unjust
self-serving
where we, the ones painted
in red and blue
both want the same thing:
to survive this hell

so it seems my friend we must wait
for each quake
each wave
each flame
to reach us
and put us out of our misery

death by a thousand cuts

I died the night you left me
I was alive in a sense
breathing, heart beating
seeing the world in color
but death had gripped me still

I died the night you left me
I had thoughts of wanting to leave
I won't lie
but you actually doing it
was like a twist of a knife

I died the night you left me
so too died 50 years of the future
and 5 years of the past
the uncertainty you gave me
killed me again and again
for days to follow

I died the night you left me
I used to be a brave soldier
undeterred by life's circumstances
I had been through so much worse
but nothing else had killed me

the way you did

I died the night you left me
and I pray everyday
that one day soon
I will be reborn

enough

you tell me I'm too much
a handful
that I cry a lot
which makes me wonder
am I even enough?

for you or for
anyone who would want
to stay and get to know
what lies behind
the tears and anger

but then I remember
my tears are from
the trauma that bonds me
and makes me kind
and the anger is for
not standing up for myself
when it actually mattered

and now instead of
wondering if I'm
too much
to you I say

enough.

cancelled

when did it become so
difficult to put to words
the ache inside me
I know you feel it too
but I fear the words I say
will fall on ears both yours
and others
who stand ready
with a self-made sword
of moral righteousness
dissecting my every
thought inspecting
my morals evaluating
my social agenda
when all I meant to say was
I am hurt
I am scared

and so again
I won't say anything
and though we could have
found solace in the fact
we both are the same

again and again
alone we will remain

the sword

when the blade strikes
and blood flows
you can scream at the steel
but the sword won't know
that was it's harsh edges
it's swift graze was
what cut you deep and
bled you to numbness

the wound is now a ghost
the knife long lost
to time
but the scar seems destined
to hold on
till death

so it does not do
to wait for closure
from the ones
who don't recognize
they were the knife that stabbed
the cause of lingering pain
the reason why

you reopen that scar
and still bleed today

butterfly

the catepillar
has no fear of the cocoon
wings are proof of hope

filtered

comparison is the thief of joy
but how do I stop measuring my life
against theirs
the ones I once knew
flaunting perfection
in filtered frames
while I stand here in my mediocrity

a degree they said would be my ticket
to the American dream
but two degrees and a decade later
unrealized dreams sit heavy
like a breath held too long
it's suffocating
but I have to keep breathing

drowning
in debt and doubt
but still I'm here
unknowingly thriving
with a family that loves me
a heart that beats strong
and a partner I'm proud to call mine

yet there's that high school girl
my rival I once bested
academically
who smiles back at me
from a photo
her life seemingly perfect
in my head she's everything
I'm not
and that voice keeps telling me
I haven't done enough
even though I want to scream
I have nothing left to give

spring

when winter's breath begins to wane
timid buds push through the frost
a whisper of warmth
passing through the air
I am no longer lost

I sit with weary eyes at rest
turned upward toward that dawning star
to catch its rays
to feel the warmth
slowly heal my skin deep scars

for so long the night ran in my veins
grief's weight pressing on my mind
winter's bitter darkness
flooding in
turning sharp what once was kind

but now spring is here at last
heat and joy must melt the snow
and like a rose on a thawed stem
I'll have my chance
again to grow

baggage

when at an airport
there are dimensions
and policies on what
we get to take to the next stop —
does it fit in a presized bag?
hidden under the seat?
any explosives, a gun?
50 pounds, 2 bags max
extra money for extra luggage

but what about the baggage
that we take with us
from milestone to milestone?
the rule I apparently follow
im allowed the entirety
of my traumatic archives
to put on display
at the next destination

but I need help every time
to move them all
for it's too much for
one person to bear

so what if I just stuck
to TSA rules I wonder —
only the necessities packed
neatly and customized with
room for new treasures considered
and nothing harmful, explosive
and no excess so that I
don't lose my ability to fly

brief relief

when a mother holds her child close
as she is shaking from fear
when a held hand can calm a nervous man
while any threat lingers near

when an extra pillow added
can soothe an aching head
when a light touch of white
can change to pink the starkest red

like when a perfect shoe allows
a sore runner to keep steady his run
like when a cast on bone
is not removed till the mending is done

the potion hits my blood
every nerve begins to still
and my racing mind is quieted
no longer fatigued no longer ill

so I'll stay in this blissful state
with my anxieties at bay
until the magic wears off again
and I start over the next day

situations

still visited by a ghost
of a memory long gone
or so I had thought —
who knew
I was human enough
to feel this way

I've told so many about you
but I can't seem
to fully tell myself
what I was feeling —
not love nor naïveté
just a paradox
set up by me
and an unknowing you

a puzzle of guessed emotion
missing its final piece
making the whole thing
unusable
wasted time
pointless

darkness

don't turn off the lights
for I fear to be alone
don't turn off the lights
for I fear the unknown

what is it about
the darkness
that draws us to the light
and makes us close our eyes

what do we fear
we might see
when there is nothing
in our sights?

depressed

everything seems so
dark
darker than it's ever been
but what really has changed?
nothing
and so I guess it is true
it is in the eye
behold
here we are
halfway from the end
of a never ending cycle
darkness
a dawn fading
into a black night
in an eternal space
like the one within
should I choose
I could return
to the daylight but
something
will have changed
I won't remember

intuition

it's more of a
visceral feeling
a half formed thought
of you and me and
a future
that is blank
with a chance to explode
like sunlight
or collapse
like a dying star
it has yet to be decided
if you and me and
this life
go together
but I know you belong
here in this moment
in this space
and for that
I am grateful

blank

blank like the canvas
that awaits a masterpiece
mistakenly placed in the hands
of an amateur

blank like the blackboard
in a classroom front and center
left empty and replaced
by the latest technologies

blank like the stares of a crowd
dumfounded and in awe
by a joke that failed
to amuse their sensibilities

blank like the life
left behind by you
open to a multitude of possibilities
with no one to pursue them

on dogs

dogs will fix your life
death is the only constant
please take me instead

dear Grandma

remember when I was a child
and you pushed me away
I asked to be loved
you told me "not today"

when you taught me to hate
that I was of beautiful face
when you were racist against me
though we are of the same race

nose bleeds and vomit
my first migraine
from a child to an adult
my hate for you remains

but now i hear you're gone
though we haven't spoken for years
and yes I may still hate you
but I still shed a few tears

for the words left unspoken
the justice left unserved
but I pray that when you meet your maker
you get the karma you deserve

best friend

how easy it is for
a friend to celebrate
to reach into their wallet
and buy a trinket
you will place on a shelf and
forget
just to prove they care
but what about the ones
that pick up the phone
at 2 am when there is just
you and the night
or will hold you close
as you cry and scream
that life did you wrong
they may not spend
a dollar
but they spend their time
and that is priceless

new love

he loves me
he loves me not
but either way I cannot
blame him

for I give and give
without expectation
for I long so much to
please him

then I take too much
and overthink his words
until I hear myself
condemn him

so though words fail
I only hope he knows
how lucky I feel to
love him

hunger games

last night I cried
for the state of the union
that country that we used to be so proud of
the pledge we used to say every morning
in a moment of unity even as a child

as an adult I would be remiss
to pledge allegiance to this country
that steals our paychecks
with the promise to make our lives better
but we know all it buys
is the genocide of brown innocents

the Capitol she is saying on the screen
is a reminder that America is a democracy
but I know every person there
holds not power for the people
but power for the sake of power
and takes pride in the fame and wealth
they can hoard rather than distribute
to the people they swear to serve

it's with a heavy heart I watch
the new President

another "father" of this nation
knowing full well that there are no men
or women
actually worthy of the seat
who will ever really rise to the title
because that is not in this country's fortune

I sedate myself before this inauguration
weeping for the future that comes next
the destruction that is inevitable
at a man's hand who claims
it's through patriotism
though it's through hate
that he wields his power, privilege, and past

I am numb at this point
to what our country will do
how we steal from the earth
orphan so many across the seas
while our own children sleep hungry
and homeless and held at gunpoint
in places they should find safety

at night when I let my guard down
when I drop all of my labels
except that of human
I will cry again and again

for being complacent in this
slow encaging and mass injustice for all

the poet

the word is out
my pen proclaimed
of self-inflicted pain

hide your secrets
change yourself
don't get hurt again

www.ingramcontent.com/pod-product-compliance
Lightning Source LLC
LaVergne TN
LVHW010946200726
843509LV00013B/2301